Après Ski

Après Ski

13-Digit ISBN: 978-1-40034-067-5

10-Digit ISBN: 1-40034-067-5

This book may be ordered by mail from the publisher. Please include $5.99 for postage and handling.

Please support your local bookseller first!

Books published by Cider Mill Press Book Publishers are available at special discounts for bulk purchases in the United States by corporations, institutions, and other organizations. For more information, please contact the publisher.

Cider Mill Press Book Publishers
"Where good books are ready for press"
501 Nelson Place
Nashville, Tennessee 37214
Visit us online
cidermillpress.com

Typography: Coquette and Sofia Pro

Image Credits: Pages 61, 62, 65, 95, 96, 134, 141, 142, 146, 149, 150, 157, 158, 161, 162, 165, 166, and 169 courtesy of Cider Mill Press.

All other images used under official license from Shutterstock.com.

Front cover, back cover, and endpaper illustrations by Jo Parry.

Printed in Malaysia

24 25 26 27 28 OFF 5 4 3 2 1

First Edition

Après Ski

A COLLECTION OF OVER 100 COCKTAILS

CIDER MILL PRESS

BOOK PUBLISHERS

Contents

Introduction

Skiing is a singular pursuit, one that requires exceptional athleticism, conditioning, and focus to gracefully navigate the mountain. It is an activity that requires you to be completely in tune with yourself in order to retain the necessary amount of control.

But skiing is also a social endeavor, a beloved pastime that brings people together and creates unbreakable bonds, an activity that relationships can be built solely around.

To bridge this gap between the individual and the social, an entire culture, known as "après ski" has evolved. Part unwinding, part thawing out, part debrief, part party, the après life has become such a crucial part of the ski trip that for many what happens out on the slopes has taken a back seat in terms of what has the greatest influence on creating an unforgettable excursion to the mountains.

As that's the case, you'll want to have your ducks in a row when it comes time to pack for your trip, and make sure you've got an answer for every situation that could arise in the après hours.

Perhaps a cold snap is due during your trip and you want to make sure you've got a handful of warming elixirs to help everyone defrost once the day is done. Maybe you or someone else in your party wants to class things up a bit before bringing everyone together around the dinner table, and you need some cocktails that are a bit more refined to set the proper tone. And what happens if you're on Day 5 of the trip, and supplies and/or morale are running a little bit low? In these instances, you'll need something a little more fun to get the "after" off on the right foot, something festive or a batch cocktail that can galvanize a large group.

A spot-on response to each and every one of these possibilities resides in the following pages, allowing you to immerse yourself in the art of après, and ensure that you're always a part of the next excursion.

Winter Warmers

Unfortunately, there's no escaping the cold when you're skiing. But Father Winter's famed bite doesn't have to be so brutal—if one is properly equipped, it can be managed quite easily. These cocktail recipes are an essential part of any successful kit meant to do battle with the elements, helping you thaw out quickly and get the evening off on the right foot.

When I Come Knocking

Ingredients

2 OZ. CHIPOTLE RUM
(SEE PAGE 232)

1 OZ. CREAM OF COCONUT

1 OZ. ORANGE JUICE

4 OZ. PINEAPPLE JUICE

NUTMEG, FOR GARNISH

1 ORANGE SLICE, FOR
GARNISH

1. Place the rum, cream of coconut, orange juice, and pineapple juice in a cocktail shaker, fill it two-thirds of the way with crushed ice, and shake until chilled.

2. Pour the contents of the shaker into a glass, garnish with a dusting of nutmeg and the orange slice, and enjoy.

Whisky Story Time

Ingredients

1 OZ. SPICED RUM
(SEE PAGE 231)

1 OZ. CROWN ROYAL
WHISKY

1 OZ. BRANDY

SPLASH OF GRENADINE
(SEE PAGE 227)

1 MARASCHINO CHERRY,
FOR GARNISH

1. Place the rum, whisky, brandy, and Grenadine in a rocks glass, add ice, and stir until chilled.

2. Garnish with the maraschino cherry and enjoy.

Whisky Story Time

see page 11

Moscow Mule

Ingredients

4 FRESH MINT LEAVES

½ OZ. FRESH LIME JUICE

2 OZ. VODKA

6 OZ. GINGER BEER

1 LIME WEDGE, FOR GARNISH

1. Place the fresh mint and lime juice in a copper mug and add ice.

2. Add the vodka and top with the ginger beer.

3. Garnish with the lime wedge and enjoy.

Hot Buttered Rum

Ingredients

1 SMALL PAT OF BUTTER

1 TEASPOON BROWN SUGAR

DASH OF CINNAMON

DASH OF NUTMEG

DASH OF ORANGE ZEST

SPLASH OF PURE VANILLA EXTRACT

6 OZ. BOILING WATER

2 OZ. AGED RUM

1 CINNAMON STICK, FOR GARNISH

1. Place the butter, brown sugar, cinnamon, nutmeg, and orange zest in a mug and stir to combine.

2. Add the vanilla extract, water, and rum and stir to combine.

3. Taste and adjust the seasoning as necessary.

4. Garnish with the cinnamon stick and enjoy.

A Stranger In The Alps

Ingredients

2 OZ. GIN

1 OZ. SIMPLE SYRUP
(SEE PAGE 223)

½ OZ. FRESH LEMON JUICE

6 OZ. FRESHLY BREWED
MINT TEA

FRESH MINT, FOR GARNISH

1 LEMON SLICE, FOR
GARNISH

1. Place the gin, syrup, and lemon juice in a mug and stir to combine.

2. Add the tea and stir to combine.

3. Garnish with fresh mint and a slice of lemon and enjoy.

Girl From The North Country

Ingredients

1 OZ. SCOTCH WHISKY

2 OZ. KAHLÚA

2 OZ. CRÈME DE CACAO

1 OZ. FRESHLY BREWED ESPRESSO OR STRONG COFFEE

WHIPPED CREAM, FOR GARNISH

1 CINNAMON STICK, FOR GARNISH

1. Place all of the ingredients, except for the garnishes, in a mug and stir to combine.

2. Layer the whipped cream on top, garnish with the cinnamon stick, and enjoy.

A Heart So White

Ingredients

1½ OZ. IRISH WHISKEY

3 OZ. HOT APPLE CIDER

½ OZ. EARL GREY SYRUP
(SEE PAGE 230)

½ OZ. FRESH LEMON JUICE

SPLASH OF HOT WATER

2 OZ. SPARKLING WINE

1 LEMON TWIST, FOR
GARNISH

1. Place the whiskey, cider, syrup, and lemon juice in a mug and stir to combine.

2. Add the splash of hot water, stir, and top with the sparkling wine.

3. Garnish with the lemon twist and enjoy.

Muleskinner Blues

Ingredients

2 OZ. TENNESSEE WHISKEY

¼ OZ. FRESH LIME JUICE

6 OZ. GINGER BEER

1 LIME WHEEL, FOR GARNISH

1 SPRIG OF FRESH MINT, FOR GARNISH

1. Pour the whiskey, lime juice, and ginger beer over ice into a glass and stir until chilled.

2. Garnish with the lime wheel and fresh mint and enjoy.

Skating

Ingredients

2 OZ. APPLEJACK

1 TEASPOON MAPLE SYRUP

6 OZ. HOT CINNAMON
APPLE TEA

1 LEMON TWIST, FOR
GARNISH

4 WHOLE CLOVES, FOR
GARNISH

1. Place the applejack, maple syrup, and tea in a mug and stir to combine.

2. Garnish with the lemon twist and whole cloves and enjoy.

Skating

see page 25

Play The Ghost

Ingredients

1½ OZ. BOURBON

¾ OZ. HONEY SYRUP
(SEE PAGE 225)

½ OZ. FRESH LEMON JUICE

DASH OF TABASCO

1 STRIP OF LEMON PEEL,
FOR GARNISH

1. Place the bourbon, syrup, lemon juice, and Tabasco in a cocktail shaker, fill it two-thirds of the way with ice, and shake until chilled.

2. Strain over ice into a rocks glass, garnish with the strip of lemon peel, and enjoy.

A Frequent Flame

Ingredients

DASH OF ANGOSTURA BITTERS

½ OZ. MAPLE SYRUP

1 OZ. ISLAY SCOTCH WHISKY

1 OZ. BOURBON

1 ORANGE TWIST, FOR GARNISH

1. Place the bitters, syrup, Scotch, and bourbon in a mixing glass, fill it two-thirds of the way with ice, and stir until chilled.

2. Strain into a coupe, garnish with the orange twist, and enjoy.

Hot Toddy

Ingredients

2 OZ. BLENDED SCOTCH WHISKY

½ OZ. FRESH LEMON JUICE

¼ OZ. SIMPLE SYRUP (SEE PAGE 223)

BOILING WATER, TO TOP

1 LEMON SLICE, FOR GARNISH

1 CINNAMON STICK, FOR GARNISH

1. Place the Scotch, lemon juice, syrup, and water in a mug and stir to combine.

2. Garnish with the lemon slice and cinnamon stick and enjoy.

Hot Toddy

see page 31

Hear The Wind Blow

Ingredients

½ OZ. FRESH LEMON JUICE

1 TEASPOON SUGAR

1 BAG OF CHAI TEA

6 OZ. BOILING WATER

1½ OZ. BOURBON

1 CINNAMON STICK, FOR GARNISH

1. Place the lemon juice, sugar, tea, and boiling water in a mug and steep for 5 minutes.

2. Remove the tea bag, discard it, and stir in the bourbon.

3. Garnish with the cinnamon stick and enjoy.

El Diablo

Ingredients

1½ OZ. SILVER TEQUILA

1 OZ. CRÈME DE CASSIS

½ OZ. FRESH LIME JUICE

GINGER BEER, TO TOP

FRESH MINT, FOR GARNISH

1. Place the tequila, liqueur, and lime juice in a cocktail shaker, fill it two-thirds of the way with ice, and shake until chilled.

2. Strain over ice into a rocks glass and top with ginger beer.

3. Garnish with the fresh mint and enjoy.

Clouds Lift

Ingredients

½ OZ. HONEY

½ OZ. MAPLE SYRUP

1 OZ. HOT WATER

½ OZ. FRESH LEMON JUICE

2 OZ. AGED RUM

1 LEMON TWIST, FOR GARNISH

1. Place the honey, maple syrup, and hot water in a mug and stir until the honey and syrup have liquefied.

2. Place the lemon juice and rum in a cocktail shaker, add the honey-and-syrup mixture, and fill the shaker two-thirds of the way with ice.

3. Shake until chilled and strain into a rocks glass.

4. Garnish with the lemon twist and enjoy.

Clouds Lift

see page 37

A Cold Snap

Ingredients

1½ OZ. RUM

1½ OZ. IRISH CREAM LIQUEUR

4 OZ. HOT CHOCOLATE

WHIPPED CREAM, FOR GARNISH

COCOA POWDER, FOR GARNISH

1. Place the rum, liqueur, and hot chocolate in a mug and stir until well combined.

2. Garnish with the whipped cream and cocoa powder and enjoy.

Vampiro

Ingredients

TAJÍN, FOR THE RIM

2 OZ. MEZCAL

2 OZ. VAMPIRO MIX
(SEE PAGE 223)

½ OZ. FRESH LIME JUICE

2 OZ. FRESH GRAPEFRUIT
JUICE

¾ OZ. SIMPLE SYRUP
(SEE PAGE 223)

PINCH OF KOSHER SALT

2 OZ. SELTZER

1 CELERY STALK, FOR
GARNISH

1. Rim a pint glass with tajín.

2. Place the mezcal, Vampiro Mix, juices, and syrup in a cocktail shaker, add 1 ice cube, and shake until chilled.

3. Pour the cocktail into the rimmed glass and add the salt and seltzer.

4. Garnish with the celery stalk and enjoy.

Irish Coffee

Ingredients

3 OZ. FRESHLY BREWED COFFEE

DASH OF SUGAR

1 OZ. IRISH WHISKEY

1 OZ. IRISH CREAM LIQUEUR

WHIPPED CREAM, FOR GARNISH

1. Pour the coffee into a mug, add the sugar, and stir until the sugar has dissolved.

2. Stir in the whiskey and liqueur, garnish with whipped cream, and enjoy.

Irish Coffee

see page 43

Black Diamond

Ingredients

¾ OZ. GIN

¾ OZ. BARROW'S INTENSE
GINGER LIQUEUR

¾ OZ. FRESH LEMON JUICE

¼ OZ. HONEY SYRUP
(SEE PAGE 225)

FRESH MINT, FOR GARNISH

1. Place the gin, liqueur, lemon juice, and syrup in a cocktail shaker, fill it two-thirds of the way with ice, and shake until chilled.

2. Pour the contents of the shaker into a Collins glass, garnish with the fresh mint, and enjoy.

Arctic Warmer

Ingredients

4 OZ. HOT BLACK TEA

1 TEASPOON UNSALTED
BUTTER

1½ OZ. VODKA

½ OZ. SILVER TEQUILA

DASH OF CINNAMON

1 CINNAMON STICK, FOR
GARNISH

1. Place the tea, butter, vodka, tequila, and cinnamon in a mug and stir until combined.

2. Garnish with the cinnamon stick and enjoy.

Apple Toddy

Ingredients

2 OZ. CALVADOS

1 TEASPOON MAPLE SYRUP

3 OZ. HOT CINNAMON APPLE TEA

1 LEMON WHEEL, FOR GARNISH

1 STAR ANISE, FOR GARNISH

1. Place the calvados, maple syrup, and tea in a mug and stir to combine.

2. Garnish with the lemon wheel and star anise and enjoy.

Old Fashioned Apple Pie

Ingredients

1½ OZ. VANILLA VODKA

DASH OF DEMERARA
SYRUP (SEE PAGE 225)

3 OZ. WARM APPLE CIDER

CINNAMON, FOR GARNISH

APPLE SLICES, FOR
GARNISH

1. Place the vodka, syrup, and apple cider in a mug and stir to combine.

2. Garnish with cinnamon and apple slices and enjoy.

Old Fashioned Apple Pie

see page 51

Ring A Ding Ding

Ingredients

1½ OZ. SCOTCH WHISKY

½ OZ. COINTREAU

½ OZ. HAMILTON PIMENTO DRAM

½ OZ. ANCHO REYES VERDE POBLANO CHILE LIQUEUR

¼ OZ. DEMERARA SYRUP (SEE PAGE 225)

4 DASHES OF ANGOSTURA BITTERS

4 DASHES OF FEE BROTHERS AZTEC CHOCOLATE BITTERS

1 DEHYDRATED ORANGE WHEEL, FOR GARNISH

1. Place all of the ingredients, except for the garnish, in a mixing glass, fill it two-thirds of the way with ice, and stir until chilled.

2. Strain into a cocktail glass, garnish with the dehydrated orange wheel, and enjoy.

Walking In The Air

Ingredients

2 OZ. BOURBON

¼ OZ. SPICED SYRUP
(SEE PAGE 229)

DASH OF REGAN'S ORANGE
BITTERS

DASH OF BITTER TRUTH
ORANGE BITTERS

ZEST OF 1 ORANGE

1 ORANGE SLICE, FOR
GARNISH

1. Place all of the ingredients, except for the orange zest and garnish, in a mixing glass, fill it two-thirds of the way with ice, and stir for 20 to 30 seconds.

2. Strain over 1 large ice cube into a rocks glass, express the orange zest over the cocktail, and discard the zest.

3. Garnish with the orange slice and enjoy.

Penicillin

Ingredients

¾ OZ. HONEY & GINGER
SYRUP (SEE PAGE 226)

2 OZ. BLENDED SCOTCH
WHISKY

¾ OZ. FRESH LEMON JUICE

¼ OZ. SMOKY ISLAY SINGLE
MALT SCOTCH (LAPHROAIG
OR LAGAVULIN
RECOMMENDED)

1. Place the syrup, blended Scotch, and lemon juice in a cocktail shaker, fill it two-thirds of the way with ice, and shake until chilled.

2. Strain over ice into a rocks glass, float the single malt Scotch on top by pouring it slowly over the back of a spoon, and enjoy.

Mole Yeti

Ingredients

1 OZ. AÑEJO TEQUILA

4 OZ. LEOPOLD BROS. THREE PINS ALPINE HERBAL LIQUEUR

½ TEASPOON CHIPOTLE CHILE POWDER

6 OZ. CHOCOLATE STOUT

1. Place the tequila and liqueur in a mixing glass, fill it two-thirds of the way with ice, and stir until chilled.

2. Strain into a clean mixing glass, add the chipotle chile powder, and stir vigorously to completely incorporate it.

3. Strain into a goblet, slowly pour in the beer, and enjoy.

Sweater Weather

Ingredients

1½ OZ. AGED RUM

¾ OZ. RYE WHISKEY

½ OZ. COINTREAU

½ OZ. GINGER SYRUP
(SEE PAGE 224)

¾ OZ. FRESH LEMON JUICE

1 LEMON TWIST, FOR
GARNISH

1 WHOLE CLOVE, FOR
GARNISH

1. Place all of the ingredients, except for the garnishes, in a cocktail shaker, fill it two-thirds of the way with ice, and shake until chilled.

2. Strain over ice into a double rocks glass, garnish with the lemon twist and clove, and enjoy.

Chervona Wine

Ingredients

1½ OZ. HUNTER'S VODKA (SEE PAGE 232)

1½ OZ. DRY RED WINE

½ OZ. SWEET VERMOUTH

½ OZ. SIMPLE SYRUP (SEE PAGE 223)

1 ORANGE TWIST, FOR GARNISH

NUTMEG, FOR GARNISH

1. Place all of the ingredients, except for the garnishes, in a cocktail shaker, fill it two-thirds of the way with ice, and shake until chilled.

2. Strain over ice into a rocks glass and express the orange twist over the cocktail.

3. Garnish with the orange twist and a dusting of nutmeg and enjoy.

Cocktail Hour

Without a doubt, the après ski life is a laidback one. But it also carries a certain refined air, an elegance that you would be wise to draw out on occasion during a trip. These cocktails, a collection of classics and recent innovations that are rife with sophistication, will help you strike just the right note in these moments, providing a bit of style while still stoking the celebration.

Bloody Mary

Ingredients

½ OZ. FRESH LIME JUICE

2 OZ. VODKA

½ OZ. OLIVE BRINE

2 DASHES OF PREPARED HORSERADISH

3 DROPS OF WORCESTERSHIRE SAUCE

3 DASHES OF HOT SAUCE

DASH OF BLACK PEPPER

2 DASHES OF CELERY SALT

TOMATO JUICE, TO TOP

1. Place all of the ingredients, except for the tomato juice, in a glass, add ice, and stir until chilled.

2. Top with tomato juice and gently stir.

3. Garnish as desired and enjoy.

White Russian

Ingredients

2 OZ. VODKA

1 OZ. KAHLÚA

HEAVY CREAM, TO TASTE

1. Place a few ice cubes in a glass, add the vodka and Kahlúa, and stir until chilled.

2. Top with a generous splash of heavy cream, slowly stir until combined, and enjoy.

White Russian

see page 69

Old Fashioned

Ingredients

1 TEASPOON SIMPLE SYRUP
(SEE PAGE 223)

2 TO 3 DASHES OF
ANGOSTURA BITTERS

DASH OF WATER

2 OZ. BOURBON OR RYE
WHISKEY

1 STRIP OF LEMON PEEL,
FOR GARNISH

1 MARASCHINO CHERRY,
FOR GARNISH

1. Place the syrup, bitters, and water in a rocks glass and stir until combined.

2. Add ice and the whiskey and stir until chilled.

3. Garnish with the strip of lemon peel and maraschino cherry and enjoy.

Boulevardier

Ingredients

1 OZ. BOURBON

1 OZ. CAMPARI

1 OZ. SWEET VERMOUTH

1 STRIP OF ORANGE PEEL,
FOR GARNISH

1. Place the bourbon, Campari, and vermouth in a mixing glass, fill it two-thirds of the way with ice, and stir until chilled.

2. Strain into a coupe, garnish with the strip of orange peel, and enjoy.

Dark & Stormy

Ingredients

⅔ OZ. FRESH LIME JUICE

¼ OZ. DEMERARA SYRUP
(SEE PAGE 225)

2 DASHES OF ANGOSTURA
BITTERS

3 OZ. GINGER BEER

1½ OZ. AGED OR BLACK
RUM

1 LIME WEDGE, FOR
GARNISH

1. Place the lime juice, syrup, bitters, and ginger beer in a Collins glass, add ice, and gently stir.

2. Float the rum on top by pouring it slowly over the back of a spoon, garnish with the lime wedge, and enjoy.

Day Is Done

Ingredients

1¾ OZ. RYE WHISKEY

¾ OZ. SWEET VERMOUTH

¼ OZ. BENEDICTINE

3 DASHES OF ABSINTHE

3 DASHES OF PEYCHAUD'S BITTERS

1 MARASCHINO CHERRY, FOR GARNISH

1. Chill a coupe in the freezer.

2. Place all of the ingredients, except for the garnish, in a mixing glass, fill it two-thirds of the way with ice, and stir until chilled.

3. Strain into the chilled coupe, garnish with the maraschino cherry, and enjoy.

Let's Fall In Love Tonight

Ingredients

1 OZ. SILVER TEQUILA

¾ OZ. REPOSADO TEQUILA

¾ OZ. FRESH LEMON JUICE

⅞ OZ. HONEY WATER
(SEE PAGE 230)

1 SPRIG OF FRESH THYME,
FOR GARNISH

1 LEMON SLICE, FOR
GARNISH

1. Place all of the ingredients, except for the garnishes, in a cocktail shaker, fill it two-thirds of the way with ice, and shake until chilled.

2. Double strain over ice into a tumbler glass, garnish with the fresh thyme and slice of lemon, and enjoy.

Trinidad Sour

Ingredients

1½ OZ. ANGOSTURA
BITTERS

½ OZ. RYE WHISKEY

¾ OZ. FRESH LEMON JUICE

1 OZ. ORGEAT
(SEE PAGE 226)

1. Chill a coupe in the freezer.

2. Place all of the ingredients in a cocktail shaker, fill it two-thirds of the way with ice, and shake until chilled.

3. Strain into the chilled coupe and enjoy.

Margarita

Ingredients

SALT, FOR THE RIM
(OPTIONAL)

2 OZ. SILVER TEQUILA

1 OZ. ORANGE LIQUEUR

1 OZ. FRESH LIME JUICE

1 LIME SLICE, FOR GARNISH

1. If a rimmed glass is desired, wet the rim of a cocktail glass or coupe and coat it with salt.

2. Place the tequila, orange liqueur, and lime juice in a cocktail shaker, fill it two-thirds of the way with ice, and shake until chilled.

3. Strain over ice into the rimmed glass, garnish with the slice of lime, and enjoy.

Gin & Tonic

Ingredients

2½ OZ. GIN

2½ OZ. TONIC WATER

SPLASH OF FRESH LIME
JUICE

2 LIME WHEELS, FOR
GARNISH

1 SPRIG OF FRESH
ROSEMARY, FOR GARNISH

1. Fill a glass with ice, add the gin and tonic
water, and stir until chilled.

2. Top with the lime juice, garnish with the
lime wheels and fresh rosemary, and enjoy.

Bee's Knees

Ingredients

2 OZ. GIN

¾ OZ. FRESH LEMON JUICE

¾ OZ. HONEY SYRUP
(SEE PAGE 225)

1 LEMON TWIST, FOR
GARNISH

1. Place the gin, lemon juice, and syrup in a cocktail shaker, fill it two-thirds of the way with ice, and shake until chilled.

2. Strain into a coupe, garnish with the lemon twist, and enjoy.

Sazerac

Ingredients

⅛ OZ. HERBSAINT

1 SUGAR CUBE

3 DASHES OF PEYCHAUD'S BITTERS

1½ OZ. SAZERAC RYE WHISKEY

1 LEMON TWIST, FOR GARNISH

1. Chill a rocks glass in the freezer.

2. Remove the glass from the freezer, add the Herbsaint, and rinse the glass with it. Discard any excess and set the glass aside.

3. Drop the sugar cube in a mixing glass, add the bitters, and muddle. Add the rye along with ice, stir until chilled, and strain the cocktail into the chilled glass.

4. Garnish with the lemon twist and enjoy.

Negroni

Ingredients

⅔ OZ. CAMPARI

⅔ OZ. SWEET VERMOUTH

2 OZ. GIN

1 ORANGE SLICE, FOR
GARNISH

1. Place the Campari, sweet vermouth, and gin in a mixing glass, fill the glass two-thirds of the way with ice, and stir until chilled.

2. Strain over ice into a rocks glass, garnish with an orange slice, and enjoy.

Negroni
see page 91

A Weekend At Camelot

Ingredients

1½ OZ. TANQUERAY NO. TEN GIN

2 BAR SPOONS GRAND MARNIER

2 BAR SPOONS FINO SHERRY

2 DASHES OF ORANGE BITTERS

1 STRIP OF ORANGE PEEL

3 OLIVES, FOR GARNISH

1. Place all of the ingredients, except for the orange peel and olives, in a mixing glass, fill it two-thirds of the way with ice, and stir until chilled.

2. Strain into a cocktail glass. Hold the strip of orange peel about 2 inches above a lit match for a couple of seconds. Twist and squeeze the peel over the lit match, while holding it above the cocktail and taking care to avoid the flames. Discard the strip of orange peel.

3. Skewer the olives on a cocktail pick, garnish the cocktail with them, and enjoy.

Winnipesaukee Night

Ingredients

1½ OZ. GIN

1 OZ. CARPANO ANTICA
FORMULA SWEET
VERMOUTH

½ OZ. FERNET-BRANCA

1 STRIP OF LEMON PEEL,
FOR GARNISH

1. Place a large ice cube in a rocks glass and build the cocktail in it, adding the ingredients in the order they are listed, except for the garnish. Stir until chilled.

2. Express the strip of lemon peel over the cocktail, garnish the cocktail with it, and enjoy.

Bramble

Ingredients

2 OZ. GIN

1 OZ. FRESH LEMON JUICE

½ OZ. SIMPLE SYRUP
(SEE PAGE 223)

½ OZ. CRÈME DE MÛRE

FRESH RASPBERRIES,
FOR GARNISH

1. Place the gin, lemon juice, and syrup in a cocktail shaker, fill it two-thirds of the way with ice, and shake until chilled.

2. Fill a rocks glass with crushed ice and strain the cocktail over it.

3. Lace the crème de mûre on top of the drink, garnish with raspberries, and enjoy.

New Moon

Ingredients

1½ OZ. BOURBON

½ OZ. ZUCCA RABARBARO AMARO

½ OZ. DOLIN DRY VERMOUTH

¼ OZ. BENEDICTINE

DASH OF CHOCOLATE BITTERS

1. Place all of the ingredients in a mixing glass, fill it two-thirds of the way with ice, and stir until chilled.

2. Strain over 1 large ice cube into a rocks glass and enjoy.

Oaxaca Old Fashioned

Ingredients

1½ OZ. REPOSADO TEQUILA

½ OZ. MEZCAL

2 DASHES OF ANGOSTURA BITTERS

1 BAR SPOON OF AGAVE NECTAR

1 STRIP OF ORANGE PEEL

1. Place a large ice cube in a rocks glass. Add all of the ingredients, except for the strip of orange peel, and stir until chilled.

2. Hold the strip of orange peel about 2 inches above a lit match for a couple of seconds. Twist and squeeze the peel over the lit match, while holding it above the cocktail and taking care to avoid the flames.

3. Rub the torched peel around the rim of the glass, drop it into the drink, and enjoy.

Espresso Martini

Ingredients

1 OZ. GREY GOOSE LA VANILLE VODKA

½ OZ. COFFEE LIQUEUR

1 OZ. FRESHLY BREWED ESPRESSO

½ OZ. SIMPLE SYRUP (SEE PAGE 223)

3 COFFEE BEANS, FOR GARNISH

1. Chill a coupe in the freezer.

2. Place all of the ingredients, except for the coffee beans, in a cocktail shaker, fill it halfway with ice, and shake until chilled.

3. Strain into the chilled coupe, garnish with the coffee beans, and enjoy.

Martini

Ingredients

3 OZ. LONDON DRY GIN

½ OZ. DRY VERMOUTH

1 LEMON TWIST, FOR
GARNISH (OPTIONAL)

3 OLIVES, FOR GARNISH
(OPTIONAL)

1. Chill a cocktail glass in the freezer.

2. Place the gin and vermouth in a mixing glass, fill it two-thirds of the way with ice, and stir until chilled.

3. Strain into the chilled cocktail glass, garnish with a lemon twist or 3 olives, and enjoy.

Early Night

Ingredients

1½ OZ. SILVER TEQUILA

1½ OZ. CHERRY HEERING

½ OZ. FRESH LIME JUICE

3 OZ. ORANGE JUICE

1 MARASCHINO CHERRY, FOR GARNISH

1. Place the tequila, liqueur, and juices in a cocktail shaker, fill it two-thirds of the way with ice, and shake until chilled.

2. Fill a tumbler with crushed ice and strain the cocktail over it.

3. Garnish with the maraschino cherry and enjoy.

Early Night

see page 107

Cosmopolitan

Ingredients

1 OZ. VODKA

1 OZ. TRIPLE SEC

1½ OZ. CRANBERRY JUICE

½ OZ. FRESH LIME JUICE

1 LEMON TWIST, FOR
GARNISH

1. Chill a cocktail glass in the freezer.

2. Place all of the ingredients, except for the garnish, in a cocktail shaker, fill it two-thirds of the way with ice, and shake until chilled.

3. Strain into the chilled cocktail glass, garnish with the lemon twist, and enjoy.

Daiquiri

Ingredients

2 OZ. LIGHTLY AGED WHITE RUM

½ OZ. FRESH LIME JUICE

½ TEASPOON CASTER SUGAR

POMEGRANATE SEEDS, FOR GARNISH

1. Chill a coupe in the freezer.

2. Place the rum, lime juice, and caster sugar in a cocktail shaker, fill it two-thirds of the way with ice, and shake until chilled.

3. Strain into the chilled coupe, garnish with the pomegranate seeds, and enjoy.

Manhattan

Ingredients

2 OZ. RYE WHISKEY

⅔ OZ. SWEET VERMOUTH

2 DROPS OF AROMATIC BITTERS

2 MARASCHINO CHERRIES, FOR GARNISH

1. Chill a cocktail glass in the freezer.

2. Place the whiskey, vermouth, and bitters in a mixing glass, fill it two-thirds of the way with ice, and stir until chilled.

3. Strain into the chilled cocktail glass, skewer the maraschino cherries on a cocktail pick, garnish the cocktail with them, and enjoy.

Gimlet

Ingredients

1½ OZ. GIN

½ OZ. FRESH LIME JUICE

1 LIME TWIST, FOR GARNISH

1. Place the gin and lime juice in a cocktail shaker, fill it two-thirds of the way with ice, and shake until chilled.

2. Strain into a cocktail glass and garnish with the lime twist.

The Grand Tetons

Ingredients

1½ OZ. APEROL

1½ OZ. CYNAR

1½ OZ. RYE WHISKEY

1 ORANGE SLICE, FOR GARNISH

1. Place all of the ingredients, except for the garnish, in a mixing glass, fill it two-thirds of the way with ice, and stir until chilled.

2. Strain over ice into a mason jar or rocks glass, garnish with the orange slice, and enjoy.

The Grand Tetons

see page 117

Vesper

Ingredients

3 OZ. GIN

1 OZ. VODKA

½ OZ. LILLET BLANC OR COCCHI AMERICANO

1 LEMON TWIST, FOR GARNISH

1. Chill a coupe in the freezer.

2. Add the gin, vodka, and Lillet or Cocchi Americano to a cocktail shaker, fill it two-thirds of the way with ice, and shake until chilled.

3. Strain into the chilled coupe, garnish with the lemon twist, and enjoy.

Brandy Alexander

Ingredients

1½ OZ. BRANDY OR COGNAC

1 OZ. CRÈME DE CACAO

¾ OZ. HEAVY CREAM

NUTMEG, FOR GARNISH

1. Chill a cocktail glass in the freezer.

2. Place all of the ingredients, except for the garnish, in a cocktail shaker, fill it two-thirds of the way with ice, and shake until chilled.

3. Strain into the chilled cocktail glass, garnish with a dusting of nutmeg, and enjoy.

Snowball

Ingredients

2 OZ. GIN

2 OZ. WHITE CHOCOLATE
LIQUEUR

SPLASH OF WHITE CRÈME
DE MENTHE

NUTMEG, FOR GARNISH

1. Chill a cocktail glass in the freezer.

2. Place the gin, liqueur, and crème de
menthe in a cocktail shaker, fill it two-thirds
of the way with ice, and shake until chilled.

3. Strain into the chilled cocktail glass,
garnish with a dusting of nutmeg, and enjoy.

Get The Party Started

We've all been there—between travel, difficult days on the slopes, and lengthy encounters with the après life, there will be moments during any ski trip when your crew's energy starts to flag, people start getting cranky, and the vibe comes perilously close to getting thrown off. These cocktails are the perfect tonic for these tenuous moments, reminding everyone that the only goal away from the slopes is having a good time.

Aperol Spritz

Ingredients

3 OZ. PROSECCO

2 OZ. APEROL

1 OZ. CLUB SODA

1 ORANGE SLICE, FOR GARNISH

1. Fill a wineglass with ice and build the cocktail in it, adding the ingredients in the order they are listed, except for the garnish.

2. Garnish with the orange slice and enjoy.

Wake-Up Cider

Ingredients

1 OZ. RYE WHISKEY

2 OZ. APPLE CIDER

1 OZ. SPARKLING CIDER

1. Pour the rye and apple cider over ice into a wineglass and stir until chilled.

2. Top with the sparkling cider and enjoy.

Isle Of View

Ingredients

2 OZ. ABSOLUT ELYX VODKA

¾ OZ. ORGEAT
(SEE PAGE 226)

¾ OZ. FRESH LIME JUICE

1 OZ. PASSION FRUIT SYRUP
(SEE PAGE 235)

PINCH OF MALDON SEA
SALT

MANGO, DICED,
FOR GARNISH

FRESH MINT, FOR GARNISH

1. Place all of the ingredients, except for the garnishes, in a cocktail shaker, fill it two-thirds of the way with ice, and shake until chilled.

2. Fill a rocks glass with crushed ice and strain the cocktail over it.

3. Garnish the cocktail with mango and fresh mint and enjoy.

Isle Of View

see page 131

Let's Groove

Ingredients

⅔ OZ. AGED RUM

⅓ OZ. ELDERFLOWER
LIQUEUR

1¼ TEASPOONS FRESH
LIME JUICE

2 DASHES OF PEYCHAUD'S
BITTERS

BRUT CHAMPAGNE, TO TOP

1 STRIP OF LEMON PEEL,
FOR GARNISH

1. Place all of the ingredients, except for the Champagne and garnish, in a cocktail shaker, fill it two-thirds of the way with ice, and shake until chilled.

2. Strain the cocktail into a Champagne flute and top with Champagne.

3. Garnish with the strip of lemon peel and enjoy.

The Smoky Mountains

Ingredients

1 OZ. MEZCAL

1 OZ. SILVER TEQUILA

1 OZ. FRESH LIME JUICE

1 OZ. PINEAPPLE JUICE

½ OZ. AGAVE NECTAR

1 STRIP OF ORANGE PEEL,
FOR GARNISH

1. Place the mezcal, tequila, juices, and agave nectar in a cocktail shaker, fill it two-thirds of the way with ice, and shake until chilled.

2. Strain into a rocks glass, garnish with the strip of orange peel, and enjoy.

Set It Off

Ingredients

½ OZ. HIBISCUS SYRUP
(SEE PAGE 229)

¾ OZ. FRESH LEMON JUICE

¼ OZ. LUXARDO
MARASCHINO LIQUEUR

1½ OZ. MEZCAL

1. Chill a coupe in the freezer.

2. Place the syrup, lemon juice, liqueur, and mezcal in a cocktail shaker, fill it two-thirds of the way with ice, and shake until chilled.

3. Strain into the chilled coupe and enjoy.

Amelia

Ingredients

1½ OZ. VODKA

5 BLACKBERRIES

¾ OZ. ST-GERMAIN

½ OZ. FRESH LEMON JUICE

FRESH MINT, FOR GARNISH

1. Place the vodka and blackberries in a cocktail shaker and muddle.

2. Add the St-Germain and lemon juice, fill the shaker two-thirds of the way with ice, and shake until chilled.

3. Strain into a rocks glass, garnish with fresh mint, and enjoy.

Campfire S'mores

Ingredients

GRAHAM CRACKER CRUMBS, FOR THE RIM

CHOCOLATE SHAVINGS, FOR THE RIM

1½ OZ. BOURBON

1½ OZ. WHITE CRÈME DE CACAO

12 OZ. STOUT, TO TOP

1 TOASTED MARSHMALLOW, FOR GARNISH

1. Place the graham cracker crumbs and chocolate shavings in a dish and stir to combine. Wet the rim of a pint glass and dip it into the mixture.

2. Place the bourbon and crème de cacao in a cocktail shaker, fill it two-thirds of the way with ice, and shake until chilled.

3. Strain the mixture into the pint glass and top with the stout.

4. Garnish with the toasted marshmallow and enjoy.

King Of The Slopes

Ingredients

2 CUCUMBER SLICES, PLUS
1 FOR GARNISH

1 OZ. LONDON DRY GIN

1 OZ. FRESH LEMON JUICE

½ OZ. ANCHO REYES

½ OZ. MAHIKI COCONUT
RUM LIQUEUR

½ OZ. DEMERARA SYRUP
(SEE PAGE 225)

1 OZ. PINEAPPLE JUICE

1. Place the 2 cucumber slices in a cocktail shaker and muddle.

2. Add the remaining ingredients, fill the shaker two-thirds of the way with ice, and shake until chilled.

3. Fill a glass with crushed ice and strain the cocktail into it.

4. Garnish with an additional slice of cucumber and enjoy.

Home Away From Home

Ingredients

1½ OZ. GIN

¾ OZ. FRESH LEMON JUICE

⅞ OZ. HONEY BEER SYRUP (SEE PAGE 233)

½ OZ. DRAMBUIE

DASH OF CHILI OIL

2 DROPS OF ORANGE BLOSSOM HONEY

1 EGG WHITE

LAVENDER BUDS, FOR GARNISH

1. Place all of the ingredients, except for the garnish, in a cocktail shaker and dry shake for 15 seconds.

2. Add ice and shake until chilled.

3. Double strain into a coupe, garnish with lavender, and enjoy.

In The Pines

Ingredients

3 FRESH MINT LEAVES, PLUS MORE FOR GARNISH

2 OZ. GIN

1 OZ. ORGEAT (SEE PAGE 226)

¾ OZ. FRESH LEMON JUICE

2 DASHES OF ORANGE BITTERS

1 EDIBLE FLOWER BLOSSOM, FOR GARNISH

1. Place the fresh mint in a cocktail shaker and muddle.

2. Add all of the remaining ingredients, except for the garnishes, and ice and shake until chilled.

3. Fill a Collins glass with crushed ice and double strain the cocktail over it.

4. Garnish with the edible flower and additional fresh mint and enjoy.

Looking For You

Ingredients

1½ OZ. LONDON DRY GIN

¾ OZ. ROTHMAN & WINTER ORCHARD APRICOT LIQUEUR

¾ OZ. FRESH LEMON JUICE

2 DASHES OF ANGOSTURA BITTERS

1 STRIP OF LEMON PEEL, FOR GARNISH

1. Chill a cocktail glass in the freezer.

2. Place the gin, liqueur, lemon juice, and bitters in a cocktail shaker, fill it two-thirds of the way with ice, and shake until chilled.

3. Strain into the chilled cocktail glass, garnish with the strip of lemon peel, and enjoy.

The Robin's Nest

Ingredients

1 OZ. SUNTORY TOKI JAPANESE WHISKY

½ OZ. PLANTATION O.F.T.D. RUM

½ OZ. CINNAMON SYRUP (SEE PAGE 224)

½ OZ. FRESH LEMON JUICE

¾ OZ. PINEAPPLE JUICE

1 OZ. PASSION FRUIT HONEY (SEE PAGE 228)

1 OZ. CRANBERRY JUICE

1 PINEAPPLE WEDGE, FOR GARNISH

1 MARASCHINO CHERRY, FOR GARNISH

1. Place all of the ingredients, except for the cranberry juice and garnishes, in a cocktail shaker, fill it two-thirds of the way with ice, and shake until chilled.

2. Fill a Hurricane glass with crushed ice, strain the cocktail over it, and top with the cranberry juice.

3. Garnish the cocktail with the pineapple wedge and maraschino cherry and enjoy.

Glass Off

Ingredients

1 OZ. MEZCAL

¾ OZ. APEROL

⅞ OZ. FRESH LIME JUICE

½ OZ. DEMERARA SYRUP
(SEE PAGE 225)

1¼ OZ. PINEAPPLE JUICE

3 DASHES OF ABSINTHE

1 EGG WHITE

1 DEHYDRATED PINEAPPLE
SLICE, FOR GARNISH

1. Place all of the ingredients, except for the garnish, in a cocktail shaker containing no ice and dry shake for 15 seconds.

2. Fill the shaker two-thirds of the way with ice and shake until chilled.

3. Double strain the cocktail into a large coupe, garnish with the dehydrated pineapple slice, and enjoy.

Third Player

Ingredients

¾ OZ. MEZCAL

½ OZ. CACHAÇA OR UNAGED RUM

½ OZ. TOASTED BLACK CARDAMOM & CINNAMON MAPLE SYRUP (SEE PAGE 233)

½ OZ. FRESH LIME JUICE

¼ OZ. PISCO

¼ OZ. ROTHMAN & WINTER APRICOT LIQUEUR

¼ OZ. ANCHO CHILE LIQUEUR

½ OZ. ORGEAT (SEE PAGE 226)

¼ OZ. FALERNUM

2 DASHES OF BITTERMENS XOCOLATL MOLE BITTERS

PINCH OF SALT

CINNAMON STICKS, CRUSHED, FOR GARNISH

1. Place all of the ingredients, except for the garnish, in a cocktail shaker, fill it two-thirds of the way with ice, and shake until chilled.

2. Fill a rocks glass with crushed ice and strain the cocktail over it.

3. Garnish with crushed cinnamon sticks and enjoy.

Zu Zu

Ingredients

2 OZ. DIPLOMATICO RESERVA RUM

½ OZ. PLANTATION PINEAPPLE RUM

½ OZ. FRESH LIME JUICE

½ OZ. FRESH GRAPEFRUIT JUICE

½ OZ. FRESH ORANGE JUICE

1 OZ. #9 (SEE PAGE 231)

4 PINEAPPLE CHUNKS

CINNAMON, FOR GARNISH

1 STRIP OF ORANGE PEEL, FOR GARNISH

1. Place all of the ingredients, except for the garnishes, in a blender, add ½ cup ice, and puree until smooth.

2. Pour the cocktail into a brandy snifter, garnish with a dusting of cinnamon and the orange peel, and enjoy.

The Expedition

Ingredients

2 OZ. HAMILTON GUYANA
86 RUM

1 OZ. BOURBON

¼ OZ. COFFEE LIQUEUR

1 OZ. FRESH LIME JUICE

½ OZ. CINNAMON SYRUP
(SEE PAGE 224)

½ OZ. HONEY SYRUP
(SEE PAGE 225)

¼ OZ. VANILLA SYRUP
(SEE PAGE 230)

2 OZ. SELTZER

1 EDIBLE ORCHID
BLOSSOM, FOR GARNISH

1. Place all of the ingredients, except for the garnish, in a cocktail shaker, add crushed ice, and shake until chilled.

2. Pour the contents of the shaker into a tiki mug.

3. Garnish with the edible orchid and enjoy.

Rum Ba Ba

Ingredients

1½ OZ. APPLETON ESTATE RESERVE BLEND RUM

1½ OZ. HEAVY CREAM

1 OZ. ORGEAT (SEE PAGE 226)

½ OZ. FRESH LEMON JUICE

1¼ OZ. PASSION FRUIT PUREE

2 DASHES OF PEYCHAUD'S BITTERS

1 PASSION FRUIT SLICE, FOR GARNISH

FRESH MINT, FOR GARNISH

1. Place all of the ingredients, except for the garnishes, in a cocktail shaker, fill it two-thirds of the way with ice, and shake until chilled.

2. Double strain over ice into a rocks glass.

3. Garnish with the passion fruit slice and fresh mint and enjoy.

Cup Runneth Over

Ingredients

2 OZ. ABSOLUT ELYX VODKA

¾ OZ. ST-GERMAIN

¼ OZ. GINGER JUICE

¾ OZ. FRESH LEMON JUICE

¼ OZ. HIBISCUS SYRUP
(SEE PAGE 229)

1 SLICE OF FRESH GINGER,
FOR GARNISH

1 EDIBLE ORCHID
BLOSSOM, FOR GARNISH

1. Place all of the ingredients, except for the garnishes, in a cocktail shaker, fill it two-thirds of the way with ice, and shake until chilled.

2. Fill a copper cup with crushed ice, strain the cocktail over it, and top with more crushed ice.

3. Garnish with the slice of ginger and orchid blossom and enjoy.

North Of Eden

Ingredients

1½ OZ. VODKA

½ OZ. COCONUT RUM

¼ OZ. HEAVY CREAM

½ OZ. EGG WHITE

½ OZ. FRESH LEMON JUICE

½ OZ. SIMPLE SYRUP
(SEE PAGE 223)

2 DASHES OF LAVENDER
BITTERS

1. Chill a coupe in the freezer.

2. Place all of the ingredients in a cocktail shaker, fill it two-thirds of the way with ice, and shake until chilled.

3. Strain into the chilled coupe and enjoy.

All That Snow

Ingredients

1½ OZ. JIM BEAM VANILLA
BOURBON

3 OZ. HALF-AND-HALF

1 OZ. FRESH LEMON JUICE

1 OZ. EGG WHITE

SPLASH OF CLUB SODA

1 STRIP OF ORANGE PEEL,
FOR GARNISH

1. Chill a Collins glass in the freezer.

2. Place all of the ingredients, except for the club soda and garnish, in a cocktail shaker, fill it two-thirds of the way with ice, and shake until chilled.

3. Strain into the chilled Collins glass and add the club soda.

4. Garnish with the strip of orange peel and enjoy.

Love & Happiness

Ingredients

2 OZ. SINGLE MALT WHISKEY

1 OZ. AVERNA AMARO

2 OZ. DRY SPARKLING WINE

1. Chill a Champagne flute in the freezer.

2. Place the whiskey and amaro in a mixing glass, fill it two-thirds of the way with ice, and stir until chilled.

3. Strain into the chilled Champagne flute, top with the sparkling wine, and enjoy.

French 75

Ingredients

1 SUGAR CUBE

½ OZ. FRESH LEMON JUICE

1 OZ. GIN

2 OZ. CHAMPAGNE

1 LEMON TWIST, FOR GARNISH

1 MARASCHINO CHERRY, FOR GARNISH

1. Place the sugar cube in a Champagne flute and add the lemon juice.

2. Add the gin and top with the Champagne.

3. Garnish the cocktail with the lemon twist. Skewer the cherry with a toothpick, place it over the mouth of the Champagne flute, and enjoy.

It Was A Very Good Year

Ingredients

FLEUR DE SEL, FOR THE RIM

2 OZ. PREMIUM TEQUILA

1 OZ. GRAND MARNIER

1 OZ. FRESH LIME JUICE

4 OZ. CHAMPAGNE

1 LIME TWIST, FOR GARNISH

1. Rim a rocks glass with the fleur de sel and add ice to the glass.

2. Place the tequila, Grand Marnier, and lime juice in a cocktail shaker, fill it two-thirds of the way with ice, and shake until chilled.

3. Strain into the rimmed rocks glass and top with the Champagne.

4. Garnish with the lime twist and enjoy.

Great Idea

Ingredients

1½ OZ. VODKA

1½ OZ. JÄGERMEISTER

¾ OZ. FRESH LEMON JUICE

1 LEMON WHEEL, FOR GARNISH

1. Place the vodka, Jägermeister, and lemon juice in a rocks glass and gently stir to combine.

2. Add ice to the glass and stir until chilled.

3. Garnish with the lemon wheel and enjoy.

Lipstick & Rouge

Ingredients

¾ OZ. APEROL

¾ OZ. AMARETTO

¾ OZ. FRESH LEMON JUICE

3 OZ. PROSECCO

1 LEMON TWIST, FOR GARNISH

1. Place the Aperol, amaretto, and lemon juice in a cocktail shaker, fill it two-thirds of the way with ice, and shake until chilled.

2. Strain into a Champagne flute and top with the Prosecco.

3. Garnish with the lemon twist and enjoy.

Dreamflower

Ingredients

1 OZ. WHISKEY

2 OZ. APPLE CIDER

2 OZ. HARD SPARKLING
CIDER

1. Place the whiskey and apple cider in a rocks glass, add ice, and gently stir until chilled.

2. Top with the sparkling cider and enjoy.

I Feel It Starts Again

Ingredients

1 OZ. COINTREAU

1 OZ. BRANDY

3 OZ. CHAMPAGNE

1. Place the Cointreau and brandy in a cocktail shaker, fill it two-thirds of the way with ice, and shake until chilled.

2. Strain into a Champagne flute, top with the Champagne, and enjoy.

Cocktails For A Crowd

While it can definitely be fun playing bartender, bringing along a few dozen bottles so that you can be assured of pleasing everyone may not be in the cards on every excursion to the mountains. If that's the case, don't fret—these recipes show you how you can make a few batch drinks at home, come in carrying a much lighter load, and still have a great time with a big group.

Vin Chaud

Ingredients

2 (750 ML) BOTTLES OF RED WINE

2 STAR ANISE PODS

2-INCH PIECE OF FRESH GINGER, CHOPPED

5 WHOLE CLOVES

3 CARDAMOM PODS, SMASHED

2 TABLESPOONS ORANGE ZEST

2 TABLESPOONS LEMON ZEST

¾ CUP HONEY

¾ CUP COGNAC

CINNAMON STICKS AND ORANGE SLICES, FOR GARNISH

1. Place all of the ingredients, except for the Cognac and garnishes, in a saucepan and bring to a simmer over medium heat.

2. Remove the pan from heat and stir in the Cognac.

3. Ladle into mugs and garnish each serving with cinnamon sticks and orange slices.

Hot Apple Cider

Ingredients

6 CUPS APPLE CIDER

3 CUPS BOURBON

5 CINNAMON STICKS

ORANGE PEELS, FOR GARNISH

1. Place the apple cider, bourbon, and cinnamon sticks in a slow cooker, cover, and cook on low for 2 hours, making sure the mixture does not come to a boil.

2. Ladle the cider into mugs, garnish each serving with an orange slice, and enjoy.

Café Mocha

Ingredients

8 CUPS WHOLE MILK

1 CUP HEAVY CREAM

½ CUP SUGAR, PLUS MORE
TO TASTE

½ CUP FRESHLY BREWED
ESPRESSO OR STRONG
COFFEE

½ LB. BITTERSWEET
CHOCOLATE, CHOPPED

1 CUP AGED RUM

1 TABLESPOON ORANGE
ZEST

½ TEASPOON FINE SEA SALT

1. Place the milk, cream, sugar, and espresso in a saucepan and warm it over medium heat.

2. Place the chocolate in a bowl. When the milk mixture is hot, ladle 1 cup of it over the chocolate and whisk until the chocolate is completely melted, adding more of the warm milk mixture if the melted chocolate mixture is too thick.

3. Pour the melted chocolate mixture into the pot of warm milk and whisk to combine. Add the rum, orange zest, and salt and stir to combine.

4. Ladle into mugs and enjoy.

Yard Sale

Ingredients

3 CUPS UNAGED RUM

1½ CUPS AGED JAMAICAN RUM

1 OZ. ANGOSTURA BITTERS

3 CUPS ORANGE JUICE

½ CUP PINEAPPLE JUICE

1 CUP TRIPLE SEC

2 OZ. GRENADINE (SEE PAGE 227)

ORANGE SLICES, FOR GARNISH

1. Place all of the ingredients, except for the orange slices, in a large punch bowl, add blocks of ice, and stir to combine.

2. Serve over ice in tumblers or Collins glasses, garnishing each serving with an orange slice.

At The Mercy Of Inertia

Ingredients

3 CUPS BOURBON

1 CUP WHOLE MILK

1 OZ. SIMPLE SYRUP
(SEE PAGE 223)

1 TEASPOON PURE VANILLA
EXTRACT

WHIPPED CREAM,
FOR GARNISH

1. Place all of the ingredients, except for the whipped cream, in a large punch bowl, add large blocks of ice, and stir until chilled.

2. Serve in coupes or over ice in rocks glasses, garnished with whipped cream.

Cozy Cabin

Ingredients

4 PEARS

2 CUPS FRESH LEMON JUICE

½ OZ. ROSEMARY SYRUP (SEE PAGE 227)

4 CUPS SCOTCH WHISKY

1½ CUPS GRAND MARNIER

SPRIGS OF FRESH ROSEMARY, TORCHED, FOR GARNISH

LIME WEDGES, FOR GARNISH

1. Place the pears, lemon juice, and syrup in a mixing bowl and muddle.

2. Transfer the mixture to a large punch bowl, add large blocks of ice, the Scotch whisky, and Grand Marnier, and stir to combine.

3. Serve over ice in rocks glasses and garnish each serving with a sprig of torched rosemary and a lime wedge.

Let It Snow

Ingredients

2 CUPS ABSINTHE

1 CUP HERBSAINT

1 CUP WHITE CRÈME DE MENTHE

2 CUPS HEAVY CREAM

½ OZ. SIMPLE SYRUP
(SEE PAGE 223)

DASH OF ORANGE
BLOSSOM WATER

1 EGG WHITE

FRESH MINT, FOR GARNISH

1. Place all of the ingredients, except for the garnish, in a blender and puree until combined.

2. Place the mixture in a large punch bowl, add large blocks of ice, and stir until chilled.

3. Serve in coupes or over ice in rocks glasses and garnish each serving with fresh mint.

Après Everything

Ingredients

4 CUPS FROZEN RASPBERRIES

2 CUPS FROZEN BLUEBERRIES

1 CUP LAVENDER SYRUP (SEE PAGE 228)

2 (750 ML) BOTTLES OF WHITE WINE, VERY COLD

FRESH MINT, FOR GARNISH

1. Place the raspberries, blueberries, and syrup in a large pitcher or punch bowl, stir to combine, cover, and refrigerate for 1 hour.

2. Divide the mixture between wineglasses or Champagne flutes and top with the wine. Garnish each serving with fresh mint.

Way Back When

Ingredients

2 NAVEL ORANGES, SLICED
THIN

¼ CUP FRESH LEMON JUICE

½ CUP GRAND MARNIER

12 RASPBERRIES

2 (750 ML) BOTTLES OF
SPARKLING WINE,
VERY COLD

1. Reserve 12 slices of orange and place the rest in a bowl.

2. Add the lemon juice and Grand Marnier, stir to combine, cover, and refrigerate for 1 hour.

3. Divide this mixture, the reserved orange slices, and the raspberries between wineglasses or Champagne flutes and top with the sparkling wine.

Nipping At Your Nose

Ingredients

3 CUPS FRESH LEMON JUICE

2 CUPS COGNAC

1 CUP SIMPLE SYRUP (SEE PAGE 223)

¼ CUP ORANGE LIQUEUR

3 CUPS PORT

LEMON WEDGES, FOR GARNISH

1. Place all of the ingredients, except for the garnish, in a punch bowl, add large blocks of ice, and stir until chilled.

2. Serve in coupes or over ice in Collins glasses and garnish each serving with a lemon wedge.

The Epiphany

Ingredients

3 CUPS ABSOLUT CITRON

1½ CUPS TRIPLE SEC

1½ CUPS WHITE
CRANBERRY JUICE

½ CUP FRESH LIME JUICE

1½ CUPS LEMON-LIME
SELTZER

FRESH MINT, FOR GARNISH

1. Place the vodka, triple sec, and juices in a large punch bowl, add large blocks of ice, and stir until chilled.

2. Add the seltzer and stir gently to combine.

3. Serve over ice in rocks glasses and garnish each serving with fresh mint.

Gath'ring Winter Fuel

Ingredients

1¾ CUPS AGED RUM OR COGNAC

¾ CUP ORANGE LIQUEUR

¼ CUP SPICED HIBISCUS SYRUP (SEE PAGE 234)

3 DASHES OF PEYCHAUD'S BITTERS

2 (750 ML) BOTTLES OF SPARKLING WINE

POMEGRANATE SEEDS, FOR GARNISH

1. Place all of the ingredients, except for the sparkling wine and garnish in a large punch bowl, add large blocks of ice, and stir until chilled.

2. Add the sparkling wine and gently stir to combine.

3. Serve over ice in wineglasses and garnish each serving with pomegranate seeds.

Egg Nog Punch

Ingredients

4 CUPS BUTTERMILK

8 CUPS WHOLE MILK

6 CUPS HEAVY CREAM

3 CUPS AGED RUM

2¼ CUPS VSOP BRANDY

1 TABLESPOON PUMPKIN SPICE

6 EGGS, YOLKS AND WHITES SEPARATED

1½ CUPS SUGAR

SALT, TO TASTE

1. In a large container, combine the buttermilk, milk, heavy cream, rum, brandy, and pumpkin spice.

2. Combine the egg yolks and 1 cup of sugar in the work bowl of a stand mixer fitted with the whisk attachment. Whisk the mixture until it is a vibrant yellow. Add the egg yolk mixture to the mixture in the large container and whisk to incorporate.

3. Clean the stand mixer's work bowl and then place the egg whites and remaining sugar in it. Whip until soft peaks form.

4. Gradually fold the egg white mixture into the liquid mixture, which will create a more luscious texture.

5. Chill the eggnog in the refrigerator for 1 hour before serving.

Sangria

Ingredients

2 (750 ML) BOTTLES OF RED WINE

1½ CUPS BRANDY

1 CUP SIMPLE SYRUP (SEE PAGE 223)

1 CUP ORANGE JUICE

2 APPLES, CORED AND DICED

2 ORANGES, PEELED AND SLICED THIN

5 LEMON WHEELS

5 LIME WHEELS

1. Place all of the ingredients in a large, airtight container and seal.

2. Chill for 24 hours to allow the flavors to combine and pour the sangria into glasses when ready to serve.

Gettin' Cozy

Ingredients

2 (750 ML) BOTTLES OF
DRY RED WINE

4 APPLES, CORED
AND DICED

2 ORANGES, SLICED THIN

½ CUP APPLE VODKA

2 CUPS APPLE CIDER

DASH OF CINNAMON

POMEGRANATE SEEDS,
FOR GARNISH

1. Place all of the ingredients, except for the pomegranate seeds, in a large, airtight container. Chill for 4 or more hours.

2. Serve over ice and garnish each serving with pomegranate seeds.

Dance Of Twinkle & Shadow

Ingredients

2 (750 ML) BOTTLES OF
DRY RED WINE

2 PLUMS, PITTED AND
SLICED

1 CUP CHERRIES, PITTED
AND HALVED

1 CUP BLACKBERRIES

½ CUP GRAND MARNIER

4 CUPS SELTZER

1. Place all of the ingredients, except for the seltzer, in a large, airtight container. Chill for 4 or more hours.

2. Add the seltzer, gently stir, and serve over ice.

Getting Figgy With It

Ingredients

2 (750 ML) BOTTLES OF DRY RED WINE

2 CUPS FRESH RASPBERRIES

6 FIGS, DICED AND FROZEN

2 CUPS FIG JUICE

1 CUP POMEGRANATE JUICE

2 CUPS SELTZER WATER

SPRIGS OF FRESH THYME, FOR GARNISH

1. Place all of the ingredients, except for the seltzer and thyme, in a large punch bowl. Chill for 4 or more hours.

2. Add the seltzer water and gently stir.

3. Serve over ice and garnish each serving with fresh thyme.

Off-Piste Punch

Ingredients

4 CUPS AGED RUM

2 CUPS BOURBON

3 CUPS SIMPLE SYRUP
(SEE PAGE 223)

4 CUPS HEAVY CREAM

NUTMEG, FOR GARNISH

1. Place the rum, bourbon, syrup, and cream in a large punch bowl, add large blocks of ice, and stir until chilled.

2. Serve in coupes and garnish each serving with a dusting of nutmeg.

Appendix

Simple Syrup

1 CUP WATER

1 CUP SUGAR

1. Place the water in a saucepan and bring it to a boil.

2. Add the sugar and stir until it has dissolved.

3. Remove the pan from heat and let the syrup cool before using or storing in the refrigerator, where it will keep for up to 3 months.

Vampiro Mix

10 OZ. CLAMATO

1 OZ. APPLE CIDER VINEGAR

3 OZ. FRESH LIME JUICE

2 OZ. AGAVE NECTAR

1 TABLESPOON SRIRACHA

2 TEASPOONS BLOOD ORANGE JUICE

2 TEASPOONS SMOKED PAPRIKA

1 TEASPOON BLACK PEPPER

1. Place all of the ingredients in a blender and pulse until combined.

2. Use immediately or store in the refrigerator.

Ginger Syrup

1 CUP WATER

1 CUP SUGAR

2-INCH PIECE OF FRESH GINGER, UNPEELED AND CHOPPED

1. Place the water in a saucepan and bring it to a boil.

2. Add the sugar and stir until it has dissolved.

3. Stir in the ginger, remove the pan from heat, and let the syrup cool.

4. Strain the syrup before using or storing it in the refrigerator.

Cinnamon Syrup

1 CUP WATER

2 CINNAMON STICKS, HALVED

2 CUPS SUGAR

1. Place the water and cinnamon sticks in a saucepan and bring the mixture to a boil.

2. Add the sugar and stir until it has dissolved. Remove the pan from heat.

3. Cover the pan and let the syrup sit at room temperature for 12 hours.

4. Strain the syrup before using or storing it in the refrigerator.

Demerara Syrup

1 CUP WATER

½ CUP DEMERARA SUGAR

1½ CUPS SUGAR

1. Place the water in a saucepan and bring it to a boil.

2. Add the sugars and stir until they have dissolved.

3. Remove the pan from heat and let the syrup cool completely before using or storing.

Honey Syrup

1½ CUPS WATER

1½ CUPS HONEY

1. Place the water in a saucepan and bring it to a boil.

2. Add the honey and cook until it is just runny.

3. Remove the pan from heat and let the syrup cool completely before using or storing it in the refrigerator.

Orgeat

2 CUPS ALMONDS

1 CUP DEMERARA SYRUP
(SEE PAGE 225)

1 TEASPOON ORANGE BLOSSOM
WATER

1 TEASPOON VODKA

1. Preheat the oven to 400°F. Place the almonds on a baking sheet, place them in the oven, and toast until they are fragrant, about 5 minutes. Remove the almonds from the oven and let them cool completely.

2. Place the nuts in a food processor and pulse until they are a coarse meal. Set the almonds aside.

3. Place the syrup in a saucepan and warm it over medium heat. Add the almond meal, remove the pan from heat, and let the mixture steep for 6 hours.

4. Strain the mixture through cheesecloth and discard the solids. Stir in the orange blossom water and vodka. Use immediately or store the orgeat in the refrigerator.

Honey & Ginger Syrup

2 CUPS HONEY

2 CUPS WATER

2⅔ OZ. FRESH GINGER, MINCED

3 OZ. FRESH ORANGE JUICE

1. Place all of the ingredients in a blender and puree until smooth.

2. Strain the syrup before using or storing in the refrigerator.

Grenadine

2 CUPS 100 PERCENT POMEGRANATE JUICE

2 CUPS SUGAR

1. Place the pomegranate juice in a saucepan and bring it to a simmer over medium-low heat. Cook until it has reduced by half.

2. Add the sugar and stir until it has dissolved.

3. Remove the pan from heat and let the grenadine cool completely before using or storing in the refrigerator.

Rosemary Syrup

1 CUP WATER

1 CUP SUGAR

4 SPRIGS OF FRESH ROSEMARY

1. Place the water in a saucepan and bring to a boil.

2. Add the sugar and rosemary and stir until the sugar has dissolved.

3. Remove the pan from heat and let the syrup cool completely.

4. Strain before using or storing.

Lavender Syrup

1 CUP WATER

1½ CUPS SUGAR

HANDFUL OF DRIED LAVENDER BUDS

1. Place the water in a saucepan and bring to a boil.

2. Add the sugar and stir until the sugar has dissolved.

3. Remove the pan from heat, stir in the lavender, and let the syrup cool completely.

4. Strain before using or storing.

Passion Fruit Honey

1 CUP HONEY

1 CUP PASSION FRUIT PUREE

1. Place the honey in a saucepan and warm it over medium heat until it is runny.

2. Pour the honey into a mason jar, stir in the passion fruit puree, and let the mixture cool before using or storing in the refrigerator.

Hibiscus Syrup

¼ CUP DRIED HIBISCUS BLOSSOMS

2 CUPS DEMERARA SYRUP
(SEE PAGE 225)

1. Place the hibiscus blossoms and syrup in a large mason jar and let the mixture steep at room temperature for 6 hours.

2. Strain the syrup and use immediately or store in the refrigerator.

Spiced Syrup

3 CINNAMON STICKS, CRUSHED

12 WHOLE CLOVES

12 STAR ANISE PODS

2 CUPS HONEY

1. Place the cinnamon sticks, cloves, and star anise in a spice grinder and grind until the spices are fine, about 1 minute.

2. Place the ground spices in a saucepan and toast them over medium heat until they are aromatic, shaking the pan continually.

3. Add the honey, bring to a boil, and then reduce the heat and simmer for 5 minutes. Turn off the heat and let the syrup cool for about 1 hour.

4. Scrape the bottom of the pan to get all of the little seasoning bits and strain the syrup through a mesh strainer or chinois, using a spatula to help push the syrup through. Use immediately or store in the refrigerator.

Vanilla Syrup

1 CUP WATER

2 CUPS SUGAR

1 VANILLA BEAN

1. Place the water in a small saucepan and bring to a boil.

2. Add the sugar and stir until it has dissolved. Remove the pan from heat.

3. Halve the vanilla bean and scrape the seeds into the syrup. Cut the vanilla bean pod into thirds and add them to the syrup. Stir to combine, cover the pan, and let it sit at room temperature for 12 hours.

4. Strain the syrup through cheesecloth before using or storing in the refrigerator.

Earl Grey Syrup

1 CUP WATER

1 CUP SUGAR

3 TEABAGS OF EARL GREY TEA

1. Place the water and sugar in a small saucepan and bring to a boil, stirring to dissolve the sugar.

2. Add the teabags, remove the pan from heat, and let the syrup cool completely. Remove the tea bags before using or storing in the refrigerator.

Honey Water

1 CUP WILDFLOWER HONEY

1 CUP WARM WATER

1. Place the ingredients in a mason jar, stir to combine, and let the mixture cool completely before using or storing.

Spiced Rum

6 WHOLE CLOVES

1 CINNAMON STICK

6 ALLSPICE BERRIES

10 BLACK PEPPERCORNS

¼ CUP DEMERARA SYRUP
(SEE PAGE 225)

2 (750 ML) BOTTLES OF WRAY &
NEPHEW RUM

1 VANILLA BEAN

1. Place the cloves, cinnamon sticks, allspice berries, and peppercorns in a saucepan and toast them over medium-low heat until they are fragrant, about 1 minute, shaking the pan occasionally.

2. Remove the pan from heat, add the syrup and 1 tablespoon of the rum, and stir to combine.

3. Split the vanilla bean in half, scrape the seeds into the rum mixture, and add the pod as well.

4. Add enough of the remaining rum that the mixture is easy to pour, pour it into a large mason jar, and then add the remaining rum.

5. Store the jar in a cool, dark place and let the mixture steep until the flavor is to your liking.

6. Strain the rum before using or storing at room temperature.

#9

2 OZ. GINGER SYRUP (SEE PAGE 224)

1 OZ. ALMOND PASTE

1 TEASPOON ST. ELIZABETH ALLSPICE DRAM

1. Place the syrup and almond paste in a container and stir until combined.

2. Stir in the allspice dram and either use immediately or store in the refrigerator, where it will keep for up to 3 months.

Chipotle Rum

1 CUP AGED RUM

1 DRIED CHIPOTLE CHILE PEPPER, TORN

1. Place the ingredients in a mason jar and let the mixture steep at room temperature for 3 hours.

2. Strain before using or storing.

Hunter's Vodka

1½ TEASPOONS ALLSPICE BERRIES

1½ TEASPOONS JUNIPER BERRIES

½ TEASPOON BLACK PEPPERCORNS

½ TEASPOON CORIANDER SEEDS

½ TEASPOON FENUGREEK SEEDS

1 CINNAMON STICK

1 STAR ANISE POD

1 WHOLE CLOVE

1 (750 ML) BOTTLE OF VODKA

1 TABLESPOON MAPLE SYRUP

1. Place all of the ingredients, except for the vodka and maple syrup, in a dry skillet and toast over medium heat until aromatic, shaking the pan frequently.

2. Place the toasted spices in a large mason jar and add the vodka. Cover and let the mixture steep for 4 days in a dark, cool place.

3. Strain, stir in the maple syrup, and shake the bottle to combine. Chill in the freezer for 1 hour before using.

Honey Beer Syrup

1½ CUPS HONEY BEER (HONEY BROWN IS THE MOST POPULAR EXAMPLE OF A HONEY BEER)

1 CUP SUGAR

½ CUP HONEY

1. Place all of the ingredients in a saucepan and bring to a simmer, stirring until the sugar has dissolved.

2. Remove the pan from heat and let the syrup cool before using or storing in the refrigerator.

Toasted Black Cardamom & Cinnamon Maple Syrup

2 CINNAMON STICKS

3 BLACK CARDAMOM PODS

1 CUP MAPLE SYRUP

½ CUP WATER

1. Place the cinnamon sticks and cardamom pods in a dry skillet and toast over medium heat until they are fragrant, shaking the pan frequently.

2. Remove the aromatics from the pan and set them aside. Place 1 cup maple syrup and ½ cup water in a saucepan and bring to a simmer.

3. Add the toasted spices and simmer for 5 minutes. Remove the pan from heat and let the syrup cool completely.

4. Strain before using or storing in the refrigerator.

Passion Fruit Syrup

1½ CUPS PASSION FRUIT PUREE

1½ CUPS DEMERARA SYRUP
(SEE PAGE 225)

1. Place the ingredients in a mason jar, cover it, and shake until combined. Use immediately or store in the refrigerator.

Spiced Hibiscus Syrup

1 CUP WATER

½ CUP DRIED HIBISCUS BLOSSOMS OR 6 BAGS OF HIBISCUS TEA

1 CINNAMON STICK

5 WHOLE CLOVES

5 ALLSPICE BERRIES

1 VANILLA BEAN, SPLIT

¾ CUP DEMERARA SUGAR

1. Place all of the ingredients, except for the sugar, in a saucepan and bring to boil over medium heat.

2. Remove from heat and let the mixture steep for 15 to 20 minutes.

3. Strain, discard the solids, and return the liquid to the pan. Bring to a boil over medium heat and add the sugar. Stir until the sugar has dissolved, remove from heat, and let the syrup cool completely before using or storing in the refrigerator.

Metric Conversions

US Measurement	Approximate Metric Liquid Measurement	Approximate Metric Dry Measurement
1 teaspoon	5 ml	5 g
1 tablespoon or ½ ounce	15 ml	14 g
1 ounce or ⅛ cup	30 ml	29 g
¼ cup or 2 ounces	60 ml	57 g
⅓ cup	80 ml	76 g
½ cup or 4 ounces	120 ml	113 g
⅔ cup	160 ml	151 g
¾ cup or 6 ounces	180 ml	170 g
1 cup or 8 ounces or ½ pint	240 ml	227 g
1½ cups or 12 ounces	350 ml	340 g
2 cups or 1 pint or 16 ounces	475 ml	454 g
3 cups or 1½ pints	700 ml	680 g
4 cups or 2 pints or 1 quart	950 ml	908 g

Index

About Cider Mill Press Book Publishers

Good ideas ripen with time. From seed to harvest, Cider Mill Press brings fine reading, information, and entertainment together between the covers of its creatively crafted books. Our Cider Mill bears fruit twice a year, publishing a new crop of titles each spring and fall.

"Where Good Books Are Ready for Press"
501 Nelson Place
Nashville, Tennessee 37214

cidermillpress.com